TIMELESS TALES

Adventures

Retold by TANA REIFF
Illustrated by BOB DOUCET

NEW READERS PRESS

Copyright © 1993

New Readers Press
Publishing Division of Laubach Literacy International
Box 131, Syracuse, New York 13210-0131

Printed in the United States of America

9 8 7 6 5 4 3 2 1

Library of Congress Cataloging-in-Publication Data

Reiff, Tana.
Adventures / retold by Tana Reiff;
illustrated by Bob Doucet.
p. cm. — (Timeless tales)
ISBN 0-88336-458-1
1. Readers for new literates. 2. Adventure stories.
I. Doucet, Bob. II. Title. III. Series.
PE1126.A4R44   1993
428.6'2—dc20   93-12039
                                                CIP

Contents

Introduction

An adventure has danger. An adventure has risk. An adventure needs a brave person. The five stories in this book are great adventures that have been told over and over through the years.

The adventure of Gilgamesh is the first story ever written down in any language. Parts of the story were found written on different stones in an old code. Many people worked to break the code and piece together the whole story. "Gilgamesh, Who Wanted to Live Forever," is the story of a man looking for a way never to die.

The adventures of "Tom Thumb" are light stories of what happens to someone who is only as big as a thumb.

"Sinbad the Sailor" is an adventure from the tales of the *Arabian Nights*. The stories of Sinbad's sea voyages have been told for hundreds of years. It is said that they are a "grab bag" of old sailors' tales. Life at sea can be exciting, but these stories are hard to believe.

"The Twin Brothers" is a very old story from the Maya Indians of Central America. Two different sets of twins have many adventures on their way to the Underworld. But there is a different ending for each set of twins.

"The Quest for the Golden Fleece" is an old Greek myth. Jason and the Argonauts set to sea to find a special sheep's skin. It is one of the most famous adventure stories of all time.

Even now, people are having adventures. Some will write them down, or tell them to their families or friends. Maybe an adventure that is happening today will be passed on, told over and over through the years to come.

Gilgamesh, Who Wanted to Live Forever

Babylonia (an ancient land in Southwest Asia)

Gilgamesh was a king, part human, and part god. He was a strong ruler, and he was afraid of only one thing. The human side of him was afraid to die.

To keep his people and himself safe, Gilgamesh wanted to build a stone wall around his city. So he put all the men to work on it. While the men worked, Gilgamesh had fun. The men got angry with Gilgamesh. Their work was too hard, and it left them no time for their wives and children.

The men asked the gods for help. The gods decided to take Gilgamesh's mind away from the wall. To do this they made Enkidu, a wild man. He had long hair, and horns coming out of his head. He looked very mean.

Gilgamesh had never seen anything like Enkidu. "I cannot let this wild man get the better of me," Gilgamesh said to himself. So to show everyone who was king, Gilgamesh got into a big fight with Enkidu.

The two men clashed like bulls. They fought until the city walls shook. At last, Gilgamesh pushed Enkidu to the ground and held him there. Gilgamesh had won the fight.

Yet, the two men now admired each other. After all, neither had ever fought anyone so long and hard. On that day, Gilgamesh and Enkidu became best friends. And Gilgamesh forgot about his wall.

❦ ❦ ❦

A great monster had been doing terrible things to Gilgamesh's city. It set fires and made high winds that spread the fires. As each fire died out, the monster blew ashes everywhere.

Gilgamesh knew that the monster lived on the mountain of the cedar forest. But he had never seen its face. He wanted more than anything to get rid of this terrible killer.

Now that he had Enkidu, Gilgamesh was sure the time had come to face the monster. Together they climbed the mountain, armed with spears and axes. They stopped on the way to sleep, and Enkidu had a dream.

When they woke up, Enkidu told Gilgamesh about his dream. "The monster *is* the mountain," said Enkidu. "And he who first enters the cedar gate will die."

"I am not afraid," said Gilgamesh. "We shall storm the gate together!"

This they did. They did not die. As soon as they entered the cedar forest, Gilgamesh chopped down a tree. The monster felt this and showed its face. It sent trees and loose rocks down upon Gilgamesh and Enkidu. It set fires all around them.

Then the monster grabbed Gilgamesh by the hair. It swung him around and around before letting him go. Gilgamesh crashed to the ground, lucky to be alive.

Next the monster grabbed Enkidu by the horns and hit him against a tree.

Gilgamesh got back to his feet. Now was his chance to fight back. He drove his spear into the monster. Blood rolled like a river down the mountain. And the great monster fell. No longer would it trouble Gilgamesh's people.

The gods were angry at Gilgamesh for killing the monster. To punish him, they decided Enkidu must die. First he became very sick. Then he died. Gilgamesh did not understand why.

Gilgamesh was lost without his friend. He walked the desert sands for seven days. Then he went home. "I am afraid that I will die like Enkidu," he told his mother. "I must go away and learn the secret of how to live forever." And he was gone.

❦ ❦ ❦

There was a man from Gilgamesh's family who had found a way never to die. Gilgamesh headed off to find him. He hoped this Man of Life Forever would share his secret.

Gilgamesh came to twin mountains. It was said that between these mountains, the sun came in each day to light the earth. Gilgamesh saw the sun's gate before him. Two Scorpion People stood by this gate of mountain rock. They had big, biting claws and long, stinging tails. They gave off a blinding light.

"Let me in," Gilgamesh begged the guards, trying not to look at them. "I must see the Man of Life Forever."

"No one has ever seen him," said the Scorpion People.

"But I must!" cried Gilgamesh. "You must let me pass! I will do anything to see him!"

"You will not come back alive," said the Scorpion People.

"I will take my chances," Gilgamesh said.

The Scorpion People opened the rock gate. As Gilgamesh went inside the mountain, everything went black. He could see nothing as he walked. He fell over rocks. Sometimes it turned very cold. Then it would turn very hot. But always it was dark.

After nine days of this, Gilgamesh began to think he had lost his mind. A wind out of nowhere blew on his face. His heart seemed to give out. He called for help, but no one could hear him.

After 10 more days Gilgamesh spotted a tiny light ahead of him. He knew he was close to the other side of the mountain.

When he came out into the light, he found himself in a wonderful garden. The trees sparkled like rare stones. The air smelled sweet. As dark as it had been inside the mountain, it was that bright here. This garden was more beautiful than anything Gilgamesh had ever seen.

At the far end of the garden was the Bitter River. By the water's edge stood Siduri, the goddess of wine. Gilgamesh told her about his friend Enkidu and about the trip through the mountain.

Siduri felt sorry for Gilgamesh. She said, "Come. Sit down. Have a glass of wine with me."

"Tell me, please, where I can find the Man of Life Forever," Gilgamesh said as they drank. "I must learn his secret."

"You will never know how to live forever," Siduri said.

"Must I cross the river to find the Man of Life Forever?" Gilgamesh asked.

"You do not give up, do you?" Siduri laughed. "Very well. Over there you will find his boat. Perhaps his boatman will take you across."

❦ ❦ ❦

"No one alive has crossed the Bitter River," the boatman told Gilgamesh.

"I will take my chances," Gilgamesh said.

"If any water touches your skin you will die," the boatman explained. "We must be very careful. You must help me row."

They used long poles to move the boat across the river. Gilgamesh made sure that not one drop of water touched him.

On the other side, the Man of Life Forever saw the boat coming. He was angry with the boatman when Gilgamesh came up on shore.

"Why did you bring this person?" the Man of Life Forever shouted at the boatman.

"I begged him to bring me here," Gilgamesh said. "Tell me, please, why you can live forever."

"I am a special case," said the Man of Life Forever. "I saved many good people from the worst storm ever. In return, the gods gave me a great gift, to live forever."

"How can I live forever?" Gilgamesh begged to know.

"Sleep is the brother of death," said the Man of Life Forever. "Those who never die also never sleep. Perhaps, if you can stay awake for seven nights and six days, you can stay awake forever."

By this time, Gilgamesh was very tired. He tried to stay awake, but he could not. Seven nights and six days later the Man of Life Forever had to wake him.

Gilgamesh was sad that he had slept. "What shall I do now?" he asked.

"There is a magic weed at the bottom of the Bitter River," the Man of Life Forever said. "You will know this plant because it smells like a rose for miles around it. If you can get the magic weed, eat it when you reach old age. It will make you young again."

Then the Man of Life Forever turned to the boatman. "Now leave me! Take Gilgamesh back across the river and do not come back!"

❦ ❦ ❦

In the middle of the Bitter River, Gilgamesh smelled roses. He said, "I'm going under. I must get the magic weed."

"Why must you do this? You will die if you go in the river," the boatman said. "I think the Man of Life Forever is trying to trick you. You will die someday just like everyone else."

"I will take my chances," Gilgamesh said. He jumped into the river. The water was black. But the smell of roses led him to the magic weed. He pulled it out and brought it back to the boat.

"You see?" he laughed to the boatman. "I am half god! The water of the Bitter River touched me and I am still alive."

On they went. They came to a clear pool of water. Gilgamesh wanted to wash off all the black water of the Bitter River. So he waded into the pool. Just then a snake jumped from the water. It grabbed the magic weed out of the boat and ate the whole thing. Its old skin came off and new skin grew in its place.

It was true. The magic weed could make one young again. Only now there was none left for Gilgamesh.

"That was my last hope," Gilgamesh cried. "There is nothing to do but return to my home and live out the rest of my days."

❦ ❦ ❦

When Gilgamesh got home, he was very sad at first. "I have been through a great deal," he told his mother. "And yet I have not found the secret of life forever."

"Put your mind on all the good things you have done in your life," his mother said. "You had a high wall built around a great city. You got rid of the great monster of the mountain. And now you have a chance to become a better king than you have ever been."

Hearing this gave Gilgamesh some peace.

"Tell me something, my son. What have you learned?" his mother asked him.

"To enjoy life and make the best of it," Gilgamesh answered.

But Gilgamesh had one more trip to make. He went to find his friend Enkidu. He found him under the earth. Gilgamesh never felt so happy.

"We are together again," Gilgamesh cried to Enkidu. "Now that I have found you at last, how can I ever leave you?" He begged the gods to let him take Enkidu home.

The gods said, "The dead may not join the living. Only the living may join the dead."

Gilgamesh walked toward his friend Enkidu. "I must stay with you," Gilgamesh said. The earth heard him, and took him, and that was the end of his life.

Tom Thumb

England

 Back in the days of King Arthur, a man and woman lived on a mountain near the king's castle. Their life was simple, but too quiet. "I wish we had a child, even if he were no bigger than my thumb," said the man.

The Fairy Queen heard the man's wish. A short time later, the woman gave birth to a tiny baby boy. The boy was the size of his father's thumb. That was as big as he would ever be. They named him Tom Thumb.

The Fairy Queen made Tom a fine suit of clothes. From a leaf, she made him a hat, with the feather of a tiny bird for trimming. From a spider's web, she made him a shirt. From a green apple peel, she made him long stockings. From the skin of a mouse, she made him a beautiful pair of boots.

🦋 🦋 🦋

Every day Tom's mother went out to milk the cow. "Please, may I go with you?" the tiny boy asked her one day.

"I'm afraid you'll get lost," said Tom's mother.

But Tom talked her into taking him along.

He sat on a pile of hay and watched his mother milking the cow. Her eyes were on the milk pail when the cow reached out and ate some hay. Poor Tom Thumb! He found himself in the cow's mouth, along with a nice big bite of hay!

"Tom! Where are you?" his mother called when she saw that he was gone.

By that time, Tom was in the cow's stomach. He jumped around and danced like crazy. The cow didn't know what was going on inside her!

Well, what goes in one end comes out the other. That's what happened to Tom Thumb. He was a mess, but his mother was just happy he was all right. She took him home and washed him from head to toe.

🐞 🐞 🐞

When Tom's father went out to work in the field, Tom liked to go along in his pocket. One day Tom begged his father to let him drive the horse and cart.

"How can a little fellow like you drive a horse?" asked Tom's father.

"You'll see!" Tom said. "Just lift me into the horse's ear."

His father lifted Tom up and into the horse's ear.

"Go to the right!" Tom shouted to the horse. "Now turn to the left!" He called out every way to go and the horse did as Tom said.

Two men walking down the lane saw Tom when he hopped out of the horse's ear. "How much do you want for your little friend?" the men asked Tom's father.

"He's my son and he's not for sale," said Tom's father.

"Sell me," Tom whispered to his father. "Don't worry. I'll come home."

So Tom's father asked a high price. The two men paid him. "I'll ride up here on your hat," Tom told the one man. And off the three of them went.

It was much too far for Tom to jump to the ground. But the first time the two men sat down to rest, Tom spotted a mouse hole and hopped right into it.

The two men waited and waited for Tom to come back out. Night fell and Tom was still in the mouse hole. The men finally gave up and went home.

❦ ❦ ❦

As soon as Tom came out of the mouse hole, a bird came along and picked him up. The bird flew high in the sky. Tom shook his legs and arms. He made it too hard for the bird to hold on to him. Next thing Tom knew, he was falling through the sky, down into a lake.

A hungry fish saw Tom hit the water. The fish came up and ate him whole.

As luck would have it, King Arthur's men were fishing at the lake that day. They caught the fish with Tom inside it and took it to the castle for the king's dinner. What a surprise when the cook cut open the fish and found a little person inside!

King Arthur liked Tom Thumb right away. He enjoyed watching Tom dance to the court music. And when King Arthur sat at the Round Table, Tom always sat at the top of the king's chair.

But the day came when Tom wanted to go home. The king would not make him stay. "Take along as much money as you can carry," King Arthur told Tom. "And please visit me once a year."

This seemed like a good offer. However, Tom could carry no more than one penny. Even that bent his back. He began to walk home, which wasn't so far to go. But it took him two days and two nights to get there.

Tom's parents were so very happy to see him! His mother put him into the shell of a nut to keep him safe. Tom told all about his time away from home. "I'll never leave again!" he promised. "Except once a year, to visit my friend the king."

And, once a year, he did.

Sinbad the Sailor

Middle East

Sinbad was in the business of selling things.
To get the things he sold, he went off on seven
trips. He sailed the seas on great ships, but
along the way he spent much of his time
getting into and out of trouble on land. Here
are some of Sinbad's best adventures. Not only
did he become very rich, but his stories made
him famous.

 On one of Sinbad's trips, everything
was going fine until the ship was on
its way home. "Look at that green
island over there!" Sinbad called to
the captain. "Let's stop and enjoy it
before we go home."

Everyone on board cried, "Yes! Yes!" So
the captain took the ship over to the island.

It was a beautiful place, and the men
made themselves right at home. Some of
them built a fire to cook a fine dinner.

24

All of a sudden the island began to move. "What's going on here?" shouted Sinbad. The island moved again.

"Back to the ship!" called the captain. The men ran off the island and got back on board. But Sinbad was still running as the ship moved out to sea.

Just then the whole island went under water. Now Sinbad saw that this was not an island at all. It was a big, old whale. The animal had been sleeping for so long that plants had grown on its back. The men's fire had made the whale wake up and dip down into the water.

There was Sinbad, alone in the great sea around him. He kept his head up, but there was no land in sight.

Luck saved Sinbad. He saw something in the water bobbing toward him. Closer it came. Then Sinbad saw it was a wooden tub. He climbed in and floated off.

A soft wind took Sinbad and the tub to another island. Sinbad was weak and tired. The island was full of fruit trees, and there were goats for milk. In a few days, Sinbad was strong again.

Days went by, then weeks, then months. The island became Sinbad's home. Then one morning he spotted the white sails of a ship coming toward the island. As it came near, Sinbad saw that this was the ship he had been on.

"Who goes there?" the captain asked as he came to shore.

"Don't you know me? It is I, Sinbad. My hair grew long and I am very thin."

"Well, come along with us!" said the captain.

Sinbad was saved again!

🐛 🐛 🐛

On the way home, the captain stopped at another island to get fresh food and water. Sinbad set off by himself to have a look around. He grew tired and fell asleep. By the time he woke up, the ship had left without him again!

He had lived alone on an island before. He could do it again. So he walked on to see more of his new home.

As he stepped out of a clump of trees, Sinbad saw something very odd. It was large and white and almost round. "If I didn't know better, I would think it was a giant egg!" he laughed.

Just then Sinbad heard the sound of flapping wings. A giant bird flew down and sat upon the large white thing. "It *is* a giant egg!" Sinbad said. "This must be one of the giant birds I have heard people tell of!"

That gave Sinbad an idea. He climbed onto the giant bird's back. When the bird flew away, Sinbad got a ride.

The giant bird flew out over the sea toward land. It dropped Sinbad into a wide river valley, then flew away.

This land was rocky, and it was hard to walk. Then Sinbad saw what covered the land in front of him, in back of him, and to both sides. Everywhere there were diamonds! They were bigger than any diamonds Sinbad had ever seen. And there were snakes, hundreds of snakes, crawling among the shiny stones.

Sinbad watched where he walked. He reached between snakes to fill his pockets with diamonds. As he bent down, something hit him on the back. A slab of meat landed on the ground beside him. Sinbad looked up. He saw hunters at the top of the mountain, throwing meat down into the valley.

The meat stuck to the diamonds. The hunters waited above for birds to come for the meat and carry it up the mountain, diamonds and all.

One bird picked up Sinbad instead of the meat. The bird carried him to the top of the mountain. Before he knew it, Sinbad landed at the feet of the hunters.

"You have saved me!" Sinbad told the hunters. He gave them all his diamonds, then walked to a port. There, he found a ship, and off he sailed again.

❦ ❦ ❦

The ship had hardly left port when a big storm kicked up. The sea shook. The ship rocked and bumped. Water splashed on board. Everyone tried to bail out the water, but it was no use. The ship went down.

Sinbad grabbed a board from the broken ship. He held on to that board with all his might. He was the only one who lived. Again, Sinbad was lucky, but alone.

Sinbad landed on the Island of the Apes. Here, there was nothing to eat but coconuts, and they were too high to reach. Sinbad came up with an idea. He began to throw rocks at the apes up in the trees. The apes pulled coconuts off the trees and threw them at Sinbad. Before long, he had more than enough coconuts to keep him from going hungry.

Sinbad believed no other people were on the Island of the Apes. But as he ate his coconuts, an old man walked up to him.

"I have found you!" the old man said. With that, he climbed on Sinbad's back and wrapped his thin arms around Sinbad's neck.

"Get off!" Sinbad cried. But the old man stayed on Sinbad's back. Sinbad could do nothing to shake him off.

Night came, and Sinbad had to sleep with the old man on his back. Days went by, and still the old man hung on. He told Sinbad where to go and what to do. Sinbad had no choice but to do as the old man said.

One day Sinbad found grapes growing on the island. He put the juice from the grapes into a coconut shell and let it sit in the sun. The grape juice turned to wine.

"Would you care for a drink of wine?" Sinbad asked the old man.

The old man took the coconut shell and drank every drop. Now, full of wine, his arms and legs grew weak. He lost his hold on Sinbad. The old man dropped to the ground. Sinbad ran away as fast as he could.

A few days later, another ship came by. Yet again, Sinbad was saved. He told the men on board about the old man on his back.

"That, my friend, was the Old Man of the Sea," explained the captain. "No sailor has ever gotten away from him. He has tried for years to do you in. That's where all your bad fortune has come from. But you, Sinbad, are too smart and too lucky. The Old Man of the Sea will just have to wait for you until another day."

Sinbad made it home to his wife. He told his tales of adventure to his family. The stories spread so far and wide that Sinbad will never be forgotten.

The Twin Brothers

Central America (Mayan)

 There once were twin brothers who were very good at a certain ball game. They played every day, throwing a little ball through a stone ring. They never got tired of playing this game.

The Underworld was ruled by a tribe of Lords. The Lords of the Underworld enjoyed the same game the twins did. So they told the twins to come down and play.

The trip to the Underworld held one test after another for the twins. They had to cross a river of boiling water and then a river of blood. Next they came to where four roads met. One road was red. One was white. One was yellow. One was black. The black road spoke to them. It said, "Come this way."

The twins followed the black road. It took them to a large room where the Lords of the Underworld waited. Among them stood a statue that looked like one of the Lords. The twins, not knowing this was a statue, bowed to it. The Lords of the Underworld laughed at them. The sound was shocking, like a hundred echoes bouncing off the walls.

The Lords of the Underworld were still not ready to play ball. They took the twins to another room and asked them to sit on beautiful stone chairs. The twins did this, but the chairs were red hot. The Lords of the Underworld laughed.

Then the Lords of the Underworld took the twins to the House of Gloom. They walked even deeper under the earth. There, in this black cave, the twins heard the drip-drip-drip of water. All around they heard the scream of what sounded like a person. But no one was there.

The Lords of the Underworld handed each twin a torch. "Keep these torches lit until morning, or both of you will die."

The torches burned out fast. In the morning, the Lords of the Underworld killed the twins. Their heads turned into ears of corn on a stalk.

Along came a young woman. She picked an ear of corn and took a bite. As she did, the corn began to speak. It told her the story of the twins who came to play ball and became corn instead. "Leave the Underworld," the corn told the young woman. "The kernels you ate will give you sons with special power."

🐚 🐚 🐚

The young woman left the Underworld. Not long after, she became the mother of twin boys.

As this set of twins grew up, they too came to enjoy playing the ball game. The Lords of the Underworld told these twins to come down for a game.

Like their fathers, they had to cross the river of boiling water and the river of blood. They too came upon the four roads and took the black one. But these twins knew what had happened before. They were ready to face whatever the Lords of the Underworld put before them.

Like their fathers, the twins were brought to the room with the Lords and the statue. But they bowed to the real Lords and no one laughed at them.

Like their fathers, the twins were asked to sit in the stone chairs. But they said, "These chairs are too good for us. We will sit on the floor."

Like their fathers, the twins were taken to the House of Gloom. But they did not let the torches burn out. They moved the fire from one torch to the other. When morning came, they lit both torches. They were not killed.

Instead, the Lords of the Underworld played ball with them. The twins played for their lives and won the game. But the Lords would not let them go home. Not until they passed more tests.

The Lords took the twins to the House of Cold. There was ice on the walls and floor.

The twins were not afraid. There were sticks here and there on the ice floor. The twins made a pile of them. Then they rubbed the sticks together and burned the wood to keep warm.

The Lords next took the twins to the House of Cats. Two large, very mean cats lived there. On the floor lay the bones of people who had gone there before.

The twins were not afraid. They picked up the bones and threw them at the cats.

Seeing how the twins got the better of the cats, the Lords took them to the House of Bats. This was a dark cave, with only the sound of huge flying bats above.

The twins were not afraid. They lay face down on the cave floor all night. When morning came, everything was still. The twins lifted their heads, only to feel the bats flying down and ripping their skin.

The twin brothers might have died in that cave had the turtle not come along. Long ago the turtle had been a person. The Lords of the Underworld had changed him into a turtle. They did not know that this change  gave the turtle magic power. He found the twins and made their skin grow together again.

🐢 🐢 🐢

Now the twins were ready to show their own special power. They were ready to get back at the Lords for killing their fathers and for putting them through so much. So they went to the Lords and said, "Go ahead and burn us to death!"

The Lords of the Underworld laughed.
Then they set a fire and threw the twins
into it. They put the ashes into the
Underworld lake.

A few days later, two strange men were
seen walking out of the lake and around
the Underworld. They wore poor clothes.
But everywhere they went, they did magic.
The Lords began to follow them.

The strange men burned down houses
and made them come back again. They
even burned themselves and came back
again, not hurt at all.

"Make us burn and come back again, too,"
the Lords begged the two strange men.

All the people of the Underworld came
to watch. The two strange men built a great
fire. "This will be fun!" laughed the Lords of
the Underworld. Still laughing, they jumped
into the fire, heads first.

Then the laughing stopped. Everyone waited for the Lords to come back. But nothing happened.

"Where are the Lords?" the people asked.

The two strange men tore off their poor clothes. They were the twins, come back to life! They turned toward the fire and said, "We will bring you back! But no longer will you be the Lords of the Underworld. Never again will you play ball. You will never do anything but make pots and cook for everyone else. You will have no power at all!"

The twin brothers moved back from the crowd. They wanted never to see again the evil faces of the Lords of the Underworld. So before the Lords came out of the fire, the twins went home to the green earth above.

The Quest for the Golden Fleece

Greece

"Be gone with you!" said Pelias to his uncle, the king. "I am the new king!" He sent the old king to another land.

And so Pelias became the new king of Greece.

Now, the old king had a son named Jason. When Pelias became king, Jason's father sent him far away, so that he would be safe.

King Pelias ruled Greece with an iron hand. But a voice told him, "Watch out for a man wearing only one shoe." He wondered what that could mean.

Years went by. Then one day, a strange man came to see King Pelias. He wore fine clothes, and his beautiful hair went all the way down his back. But he wore only one shoe. Pelias was afraid when he saw this man.

"I am Jason, your cousin," the stranger said. "I am a man now. I am strong and brave. I have come back to Greece to become the king. I am here to take what should be mine, not yours."

"Very well," said Pelias. "But first you must bring me the skin of a golden sheep. The king of Colchis has it. You must sail there and get it. Bring it to me and you shall become the king."

❦ ❦ ❦

Jason liked the idea of a great adventure. He was happy to go to sea to get the Golden Fleece. He asked the great heroes of Greece to go with him. The group set off on a ship called the *Argo*. Everyone knew the trip would not be easy. But they had no idea just how hard it would be.

One man was lost when a mermaid grabbed him to kiss him. She pulled the man under water and he was gone forever. A second man was lost when he went under water to find the first man.

One night the *Argo* stopped on land. There, Jason and his men found an old man on the beach. He was thin and weak and could not even sit up.

"Here, take some food," Jason said to him.

As soon as Jason laid down the food, a flock of large, ugly birds flew down to the beach. Their wings were huge. Their beaks and claws were sharp. They had long, curly tails. The birds flew toward the food, touched it, then flew away. But they left behind a very bad smell. No one could eat the food once those birds had touched it.

"Now you know why I cannot eat," said the old man.

Two of Jason's men were sons of the North Wind. They flew into the sky, ready to kill the ugly birds. Just then a rainbow came out and began to speak. "Please do not kill the birds," the rainbow said. "If you leave them alone, I promise they will never again touch the old man's food."

Then Jason gave the old man more food, and he ate it in peace.

"Thank you," said the old man. "Now be on your way. But watch out for the Crashing Rocks. When you see these rocks, send a dove to fly through them. If the bird comes out alive, you will too. But if the bird is crushed, you will never get the Golden Fleece."

🐦 🐦 🐦

Before long the *Argo* came to the Crashing Rocks. These giant rocks banged against each other with great force. Jason did not see how the *Argo* could ever pass through them.

Jason held up the dove. "Fly!" he said, as he set the bird free. Jason and his men waited to see what would happen. The dove flew toward the Crashing Rocks. The rocks moved together. A feather from the bird's tail got caught between them. But she flew on and came out on the other side.

Now it was the *Argo*'s turn at the Crashing Rocks. As the rocks came apart, the ship sailed through. As soon as the ship was safe on the other side, the rocks crashed together. This time they stayed together. They never moved again, and they never hurt anyone after that day.

🌱 🌱 🌱

Next the *Argo* came to the country of fighting women. The Amazons, as they were called, were daughters of the god of war. They were always ready to fight.

Jason was ready to fight the Amazons. But just as the *Argo* came to their country, the wind began to blow. The ship blew past the country and not a drop of blood was shed.

44

At last the *Argo* reached Colchis, where the Golden Fleece was. The gods decided to help Jason get it.

The king of Colchis had a daughter named Medea. Jason did not know that Medea had magic power. She could make things happen to those she loved.

The gods sent Cupid to shoot Medea with an arrow of love. As soon as Medea saw Jason, Cupid drew his bow and shot her in the heart. She was not hurt at all. But she burned with love for Jason.

"I want the Golden Fleece," Jason told Medea's father, the king.

"I will not just give it to you," the king said. "You must work for it. First, you and your men must catch my two bulls. They are not like other bulls. They are wild, and they breathe fire. If you can get those bulls, you must use them to plow a field. Here, take these dragon teeth. Plant them in the ground. Right away they will grow into an army. If you and your men can beat that army, I will give you the Golden Fleece."

Medea heard all of this and followed Jason outside. She had never before gone against her father, but Cupid's arrow had made her ready to do anything for Jason.

Medea handed Jason a jar of special cream made from plants. "Take this," she said. "Rub the cream all over your body. No one will be able to hurt you."

Then Medea handed Jason some magic powder. "Put this powder on your spears. No one will be able to beat you."

At first Jason couldn't believe these tricks would really work. Then he looked into Medea's eyes and knew that he was safe.

"One more thing," Medea added. "When the men who grow from the dragon teeth rush toward you, throw a stone at them. They will turn against each other."

Jason and his men headed out to catch the bulls. The men shook with fear as fire shot out of the bulls' noses. But Jason walked toward the bulls without fear. He tied them to the plow and drove them across the field. One by one, the dragon teeth dropped into the ground.

As soon as all the teeth were planted, the army began to spring out of the earth and rush toward Jason and his men. Everything happened just as the king had said.

Jason remembered Medea's words. He threw a stone. It fell into the middle of the army. Sure enough, the men who grew from the dragon teeth turned against each other. In minutes, every last one of them lay dead on the ground.

🐛 🐛 🐛

The king was surprised that Jason had won. "The Golden Fleece is yours," the king told him. "However, you must get it yourself."

"I'll take you to the Golden Fleece," Medea whispered to Jason.

They walked a long way. Then Jason saw ahead of him what he had worked so hard to get. The Golden Fleece hung from the branch of a tree. Beside it was a snake, ready to kill anyone who came near.

Once again Medea used her magic power. She sang to the snake and it sank to the ground, sound asleep.

Jason took the Golden Fleece. "Come back to Greece with me," he begged Medea. "At last I shall become king. At last I shall have what was mine all along."

The *Argo,* with Medea on board, made it back to Greece safely. The gods made sure of that.